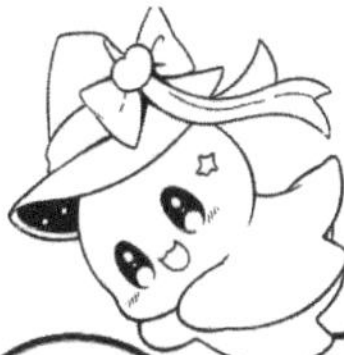

SPOOKY KAWAII

THIS BOOK BELONGS TO:

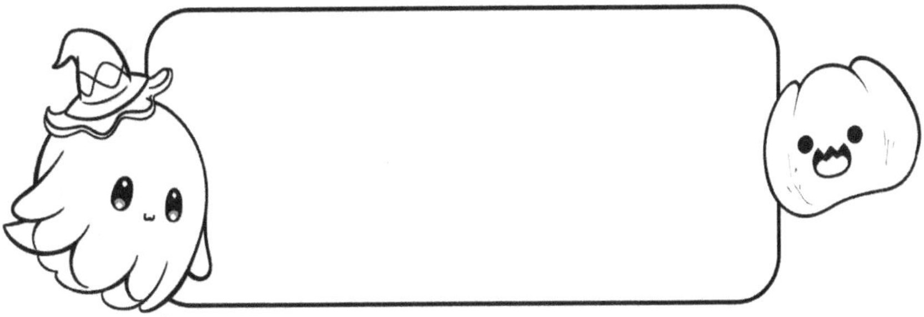

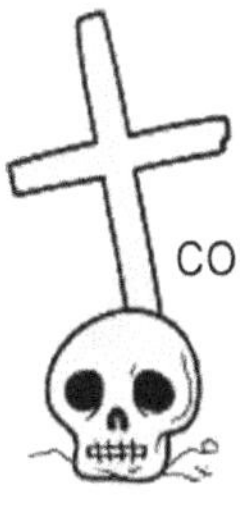

COLOR TEST

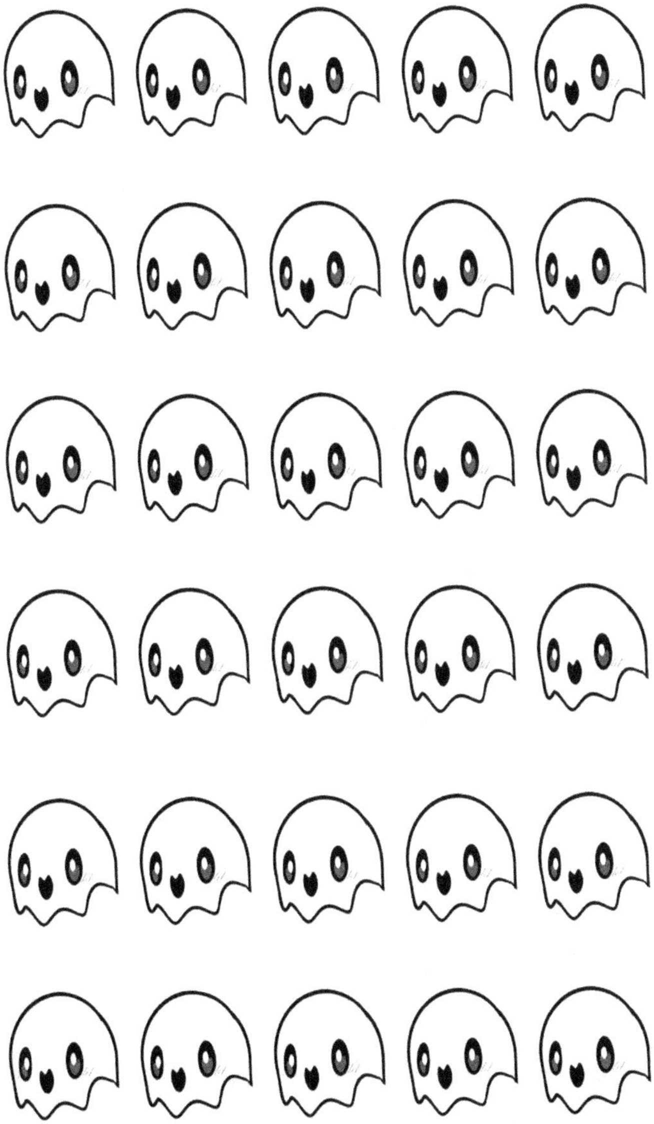

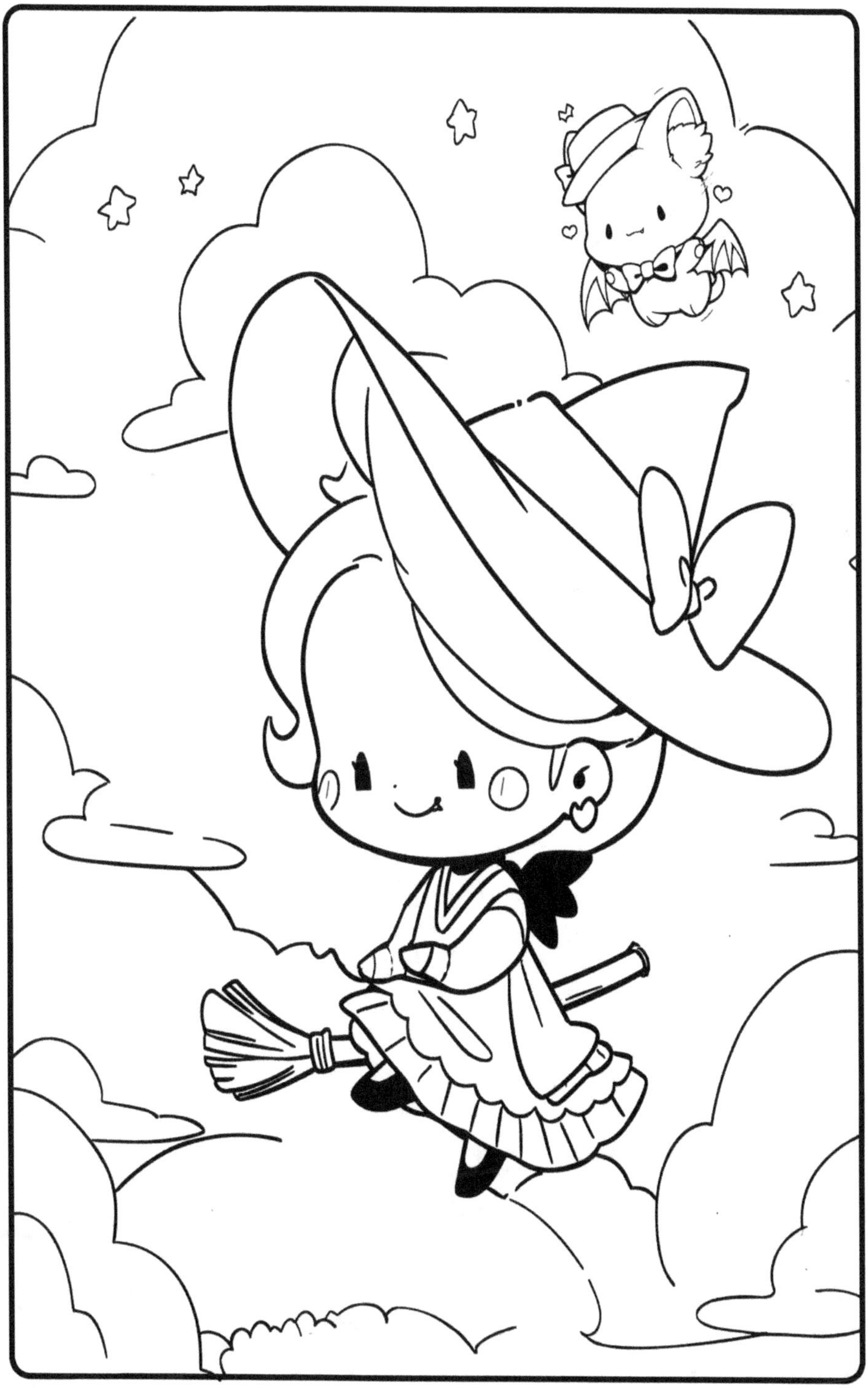

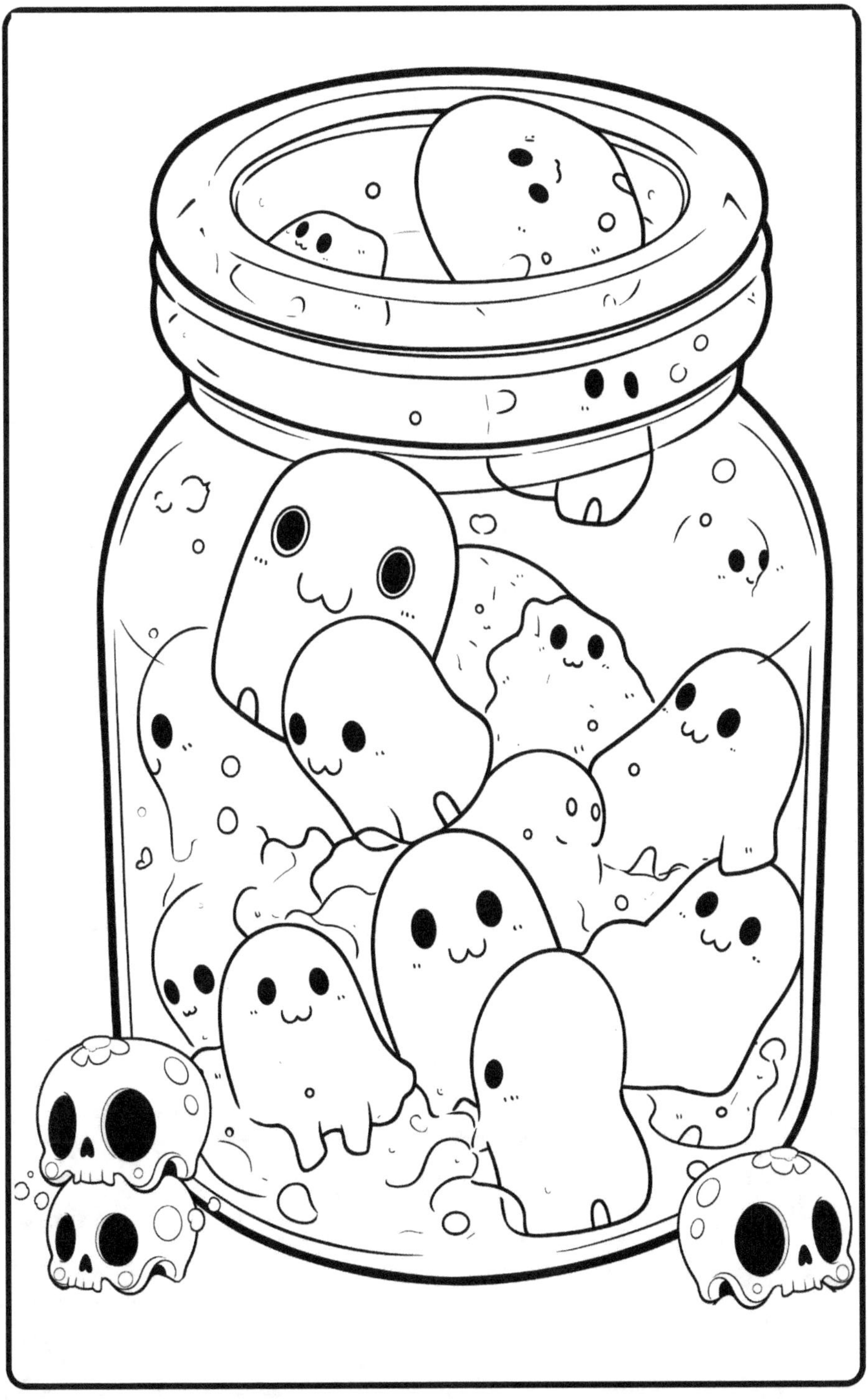

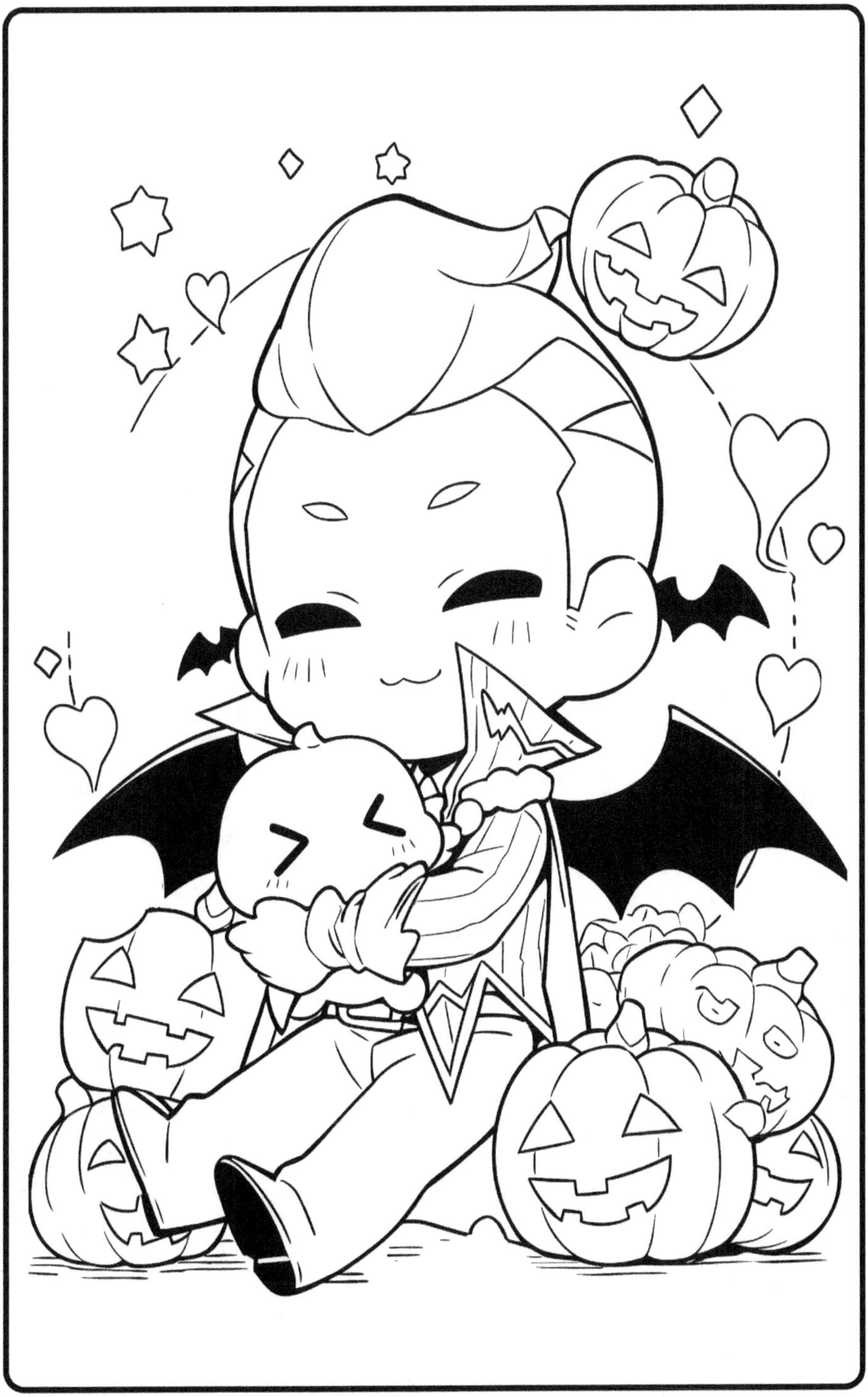

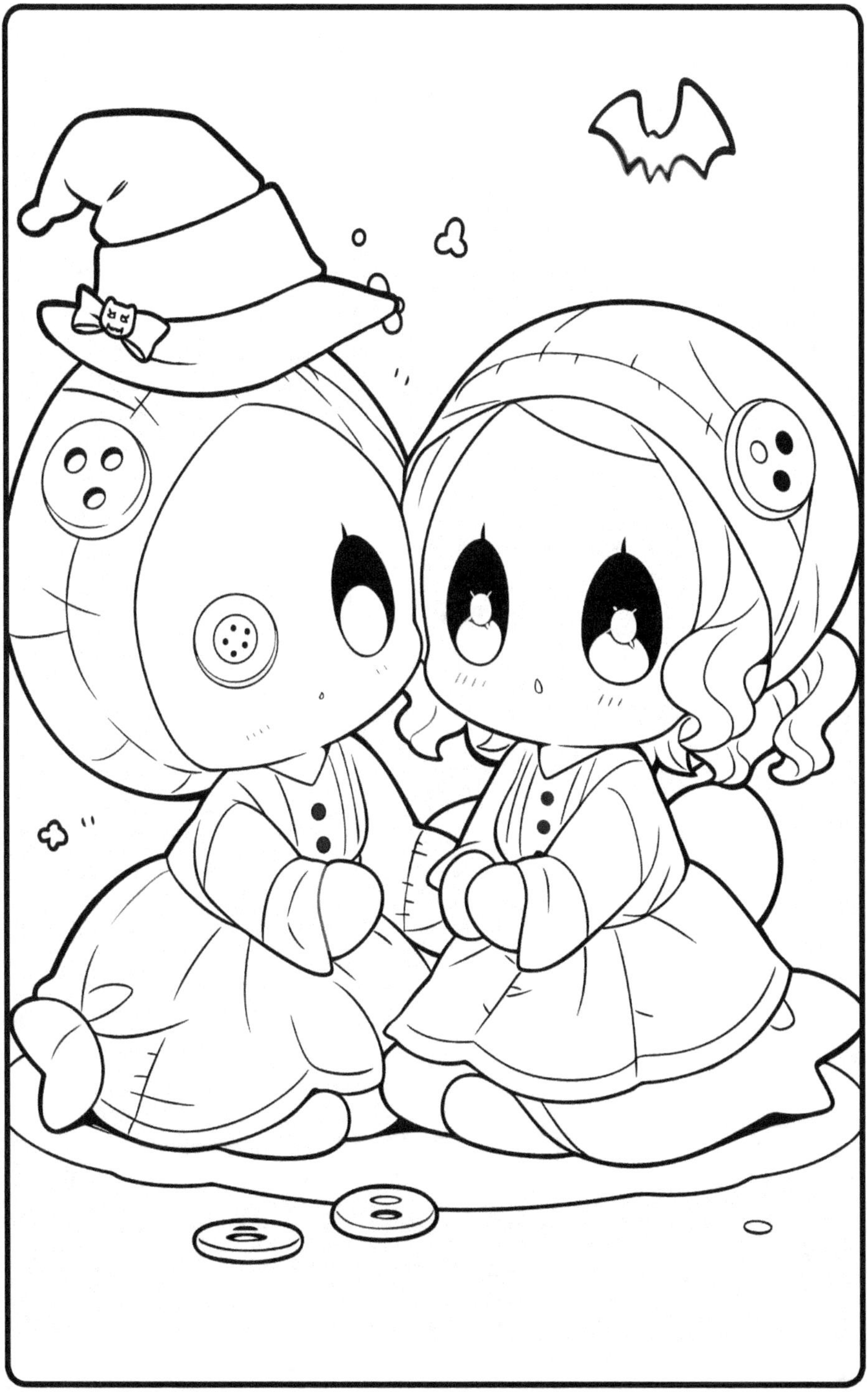

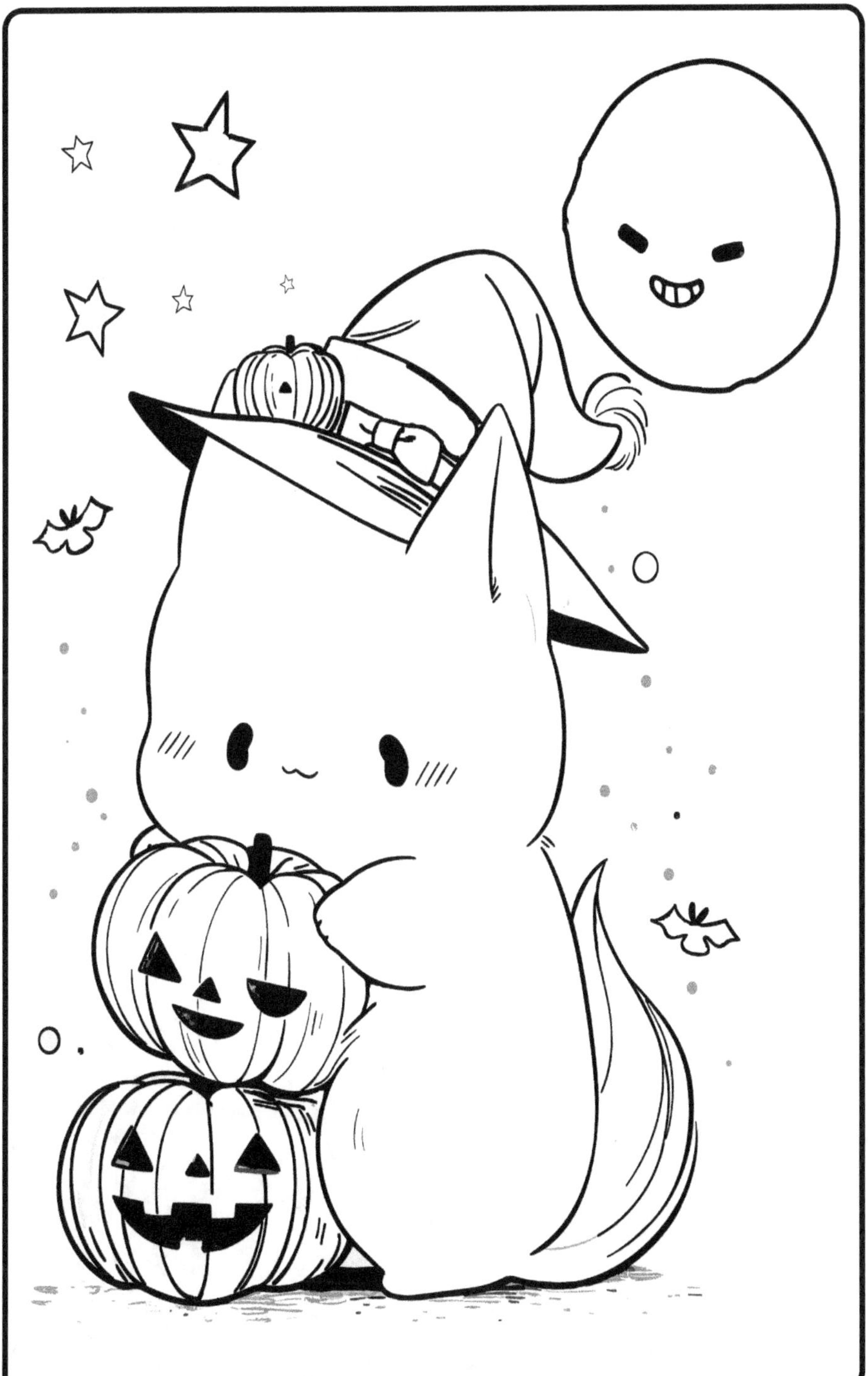

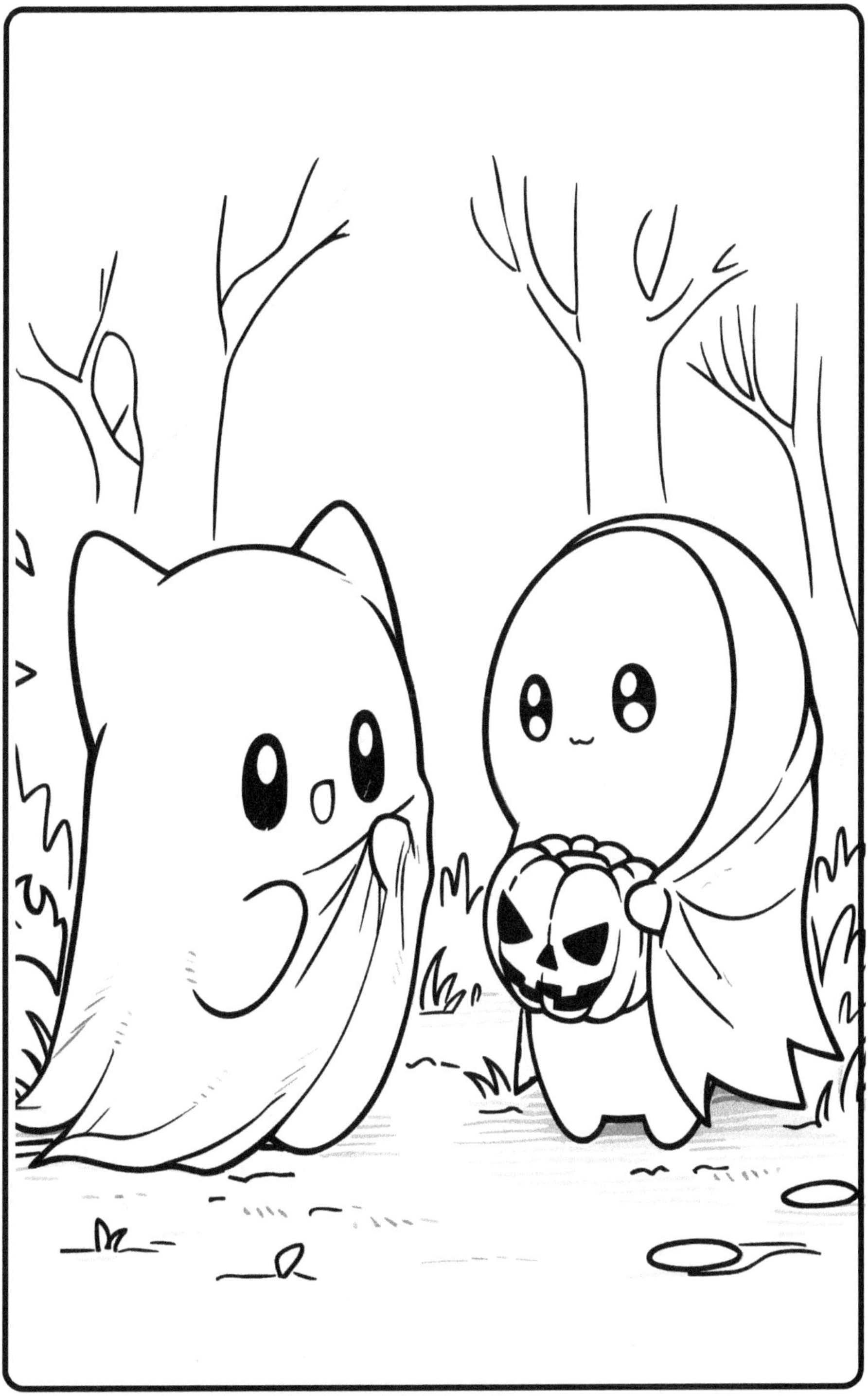

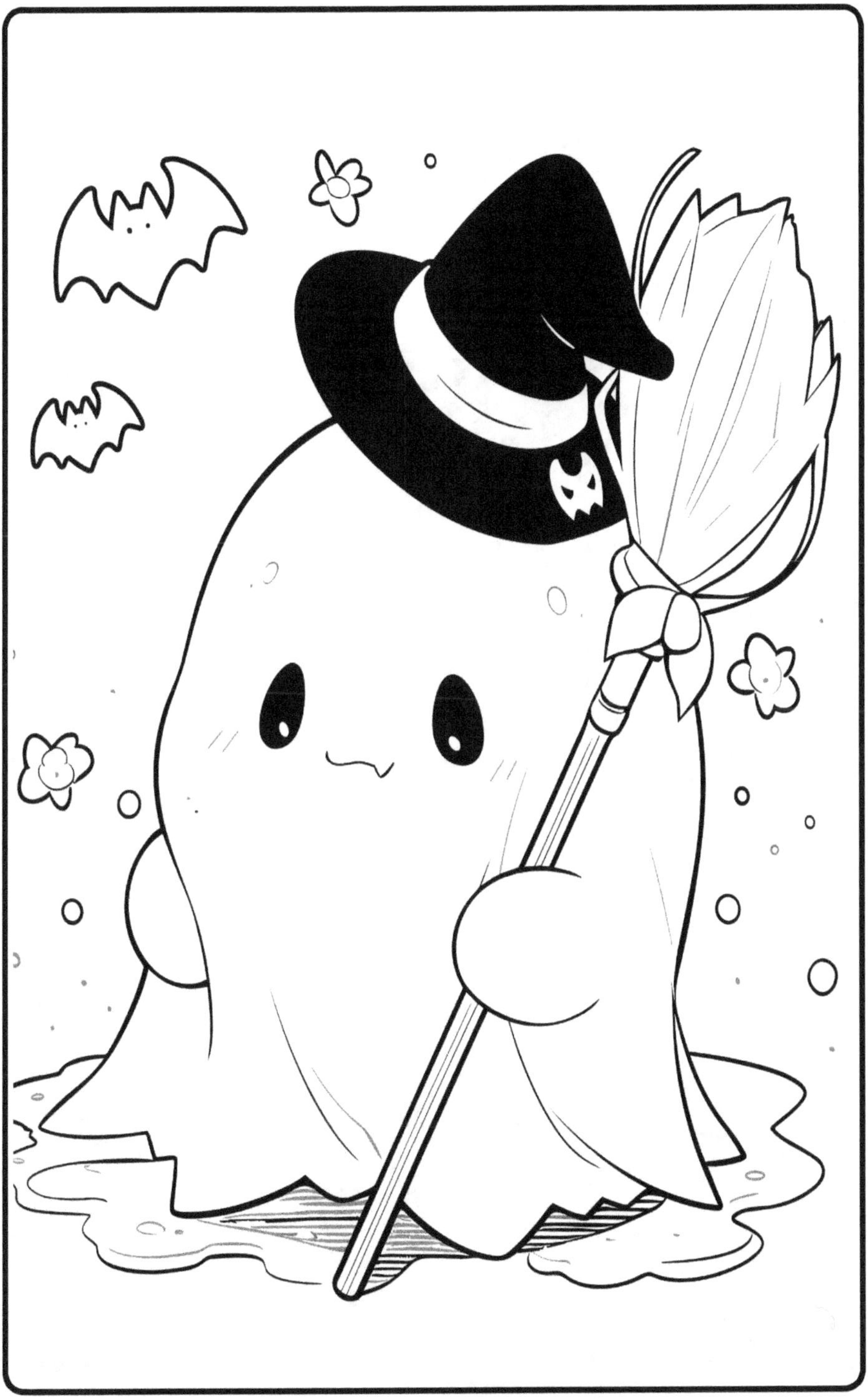

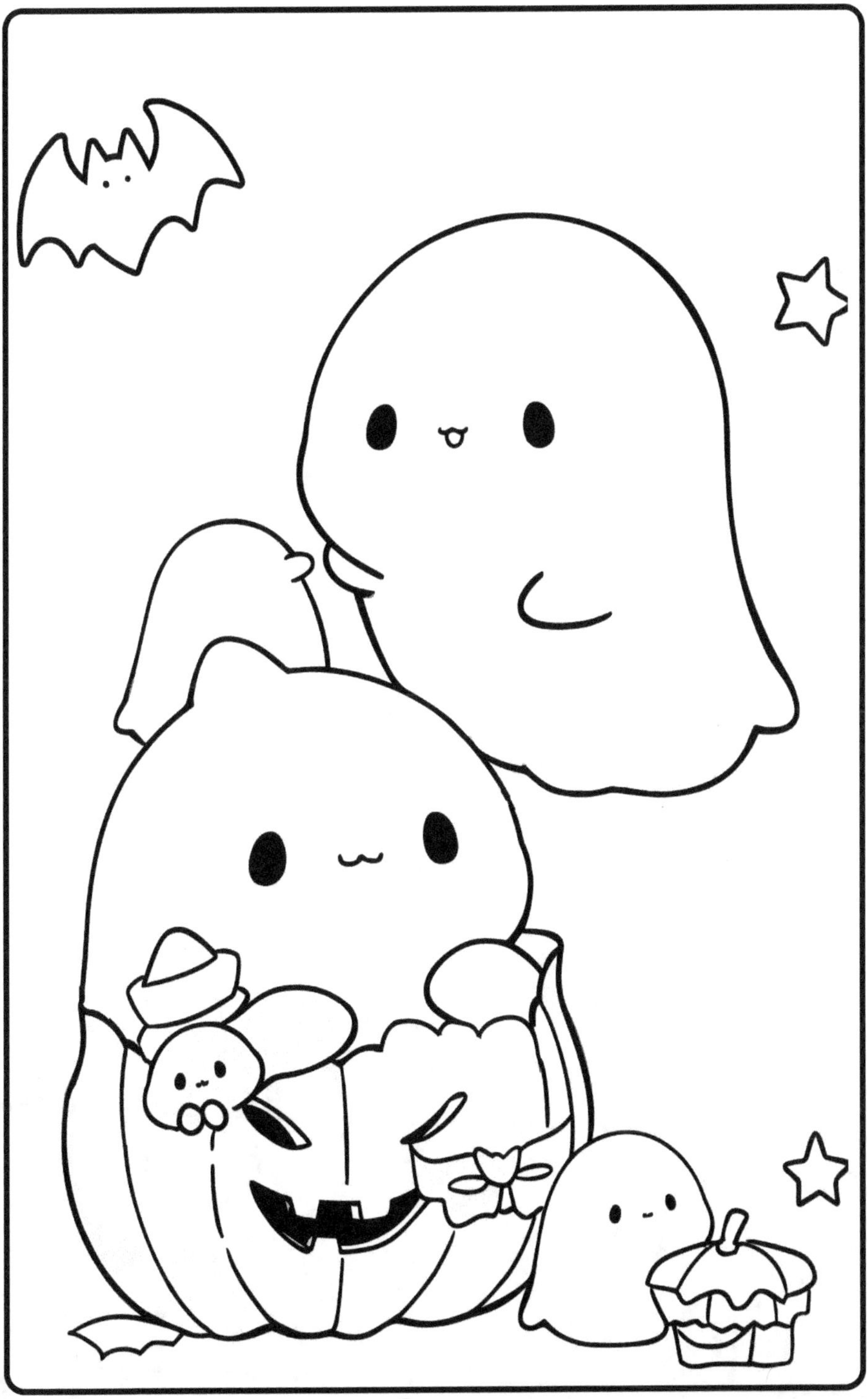

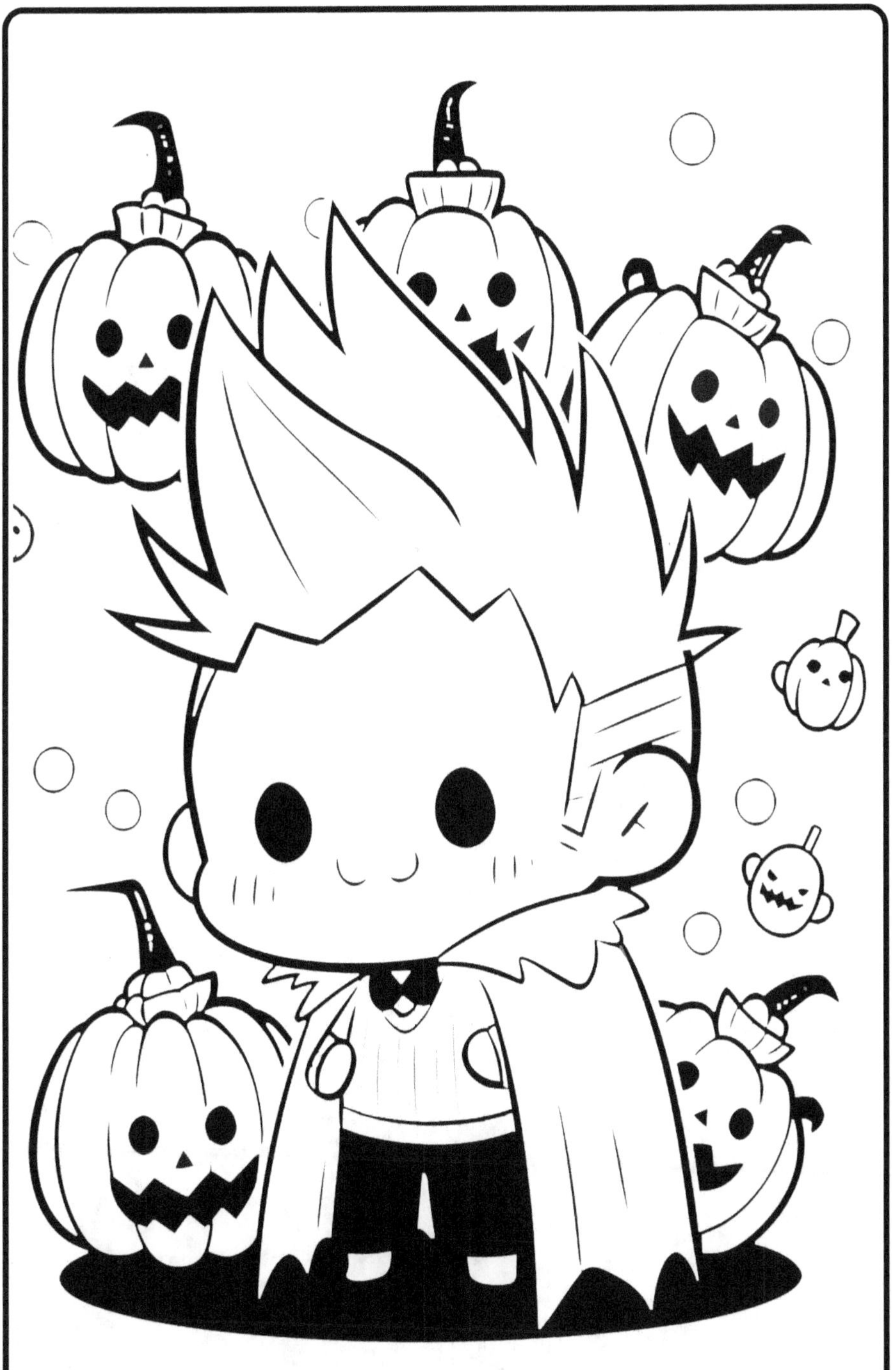

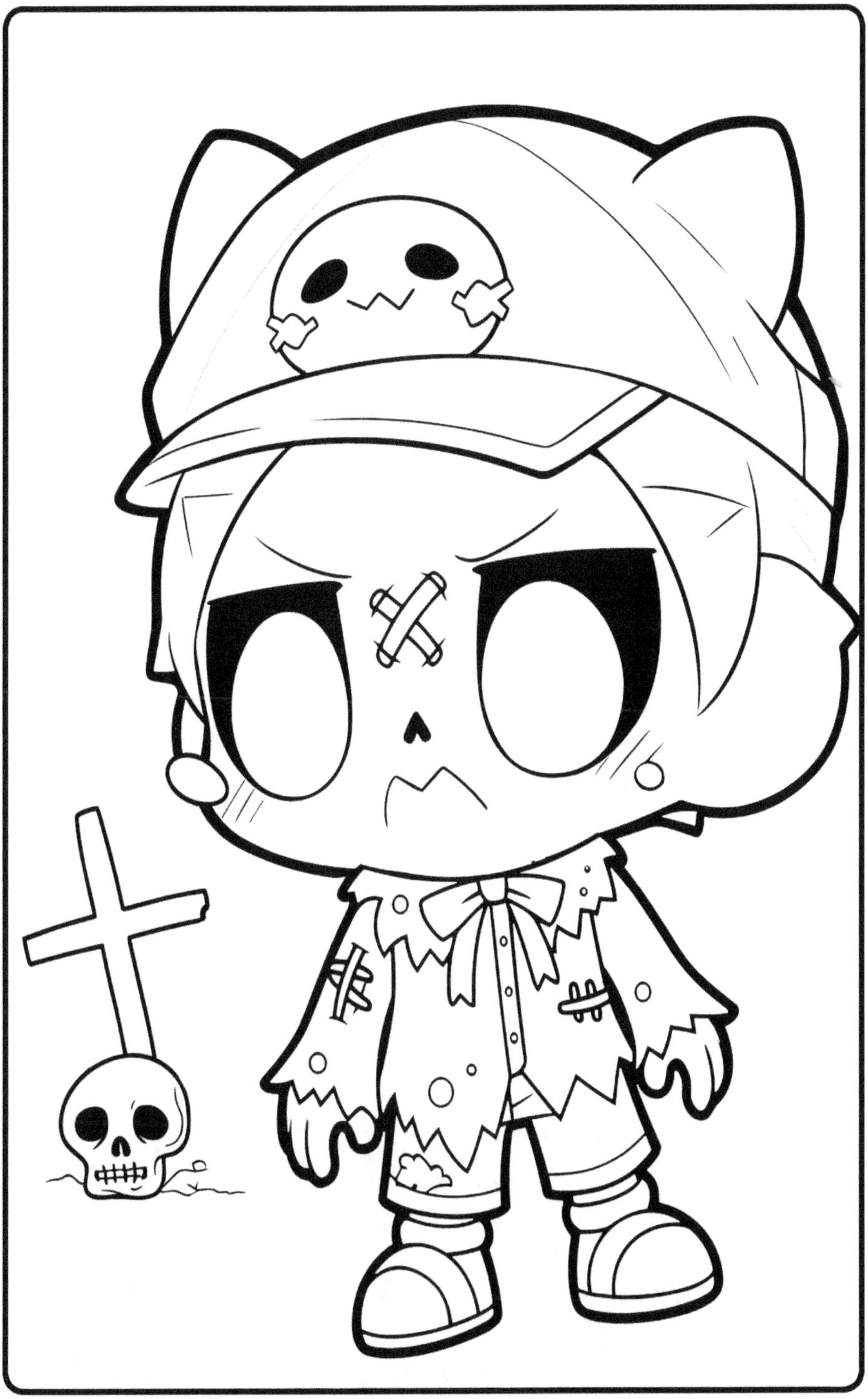

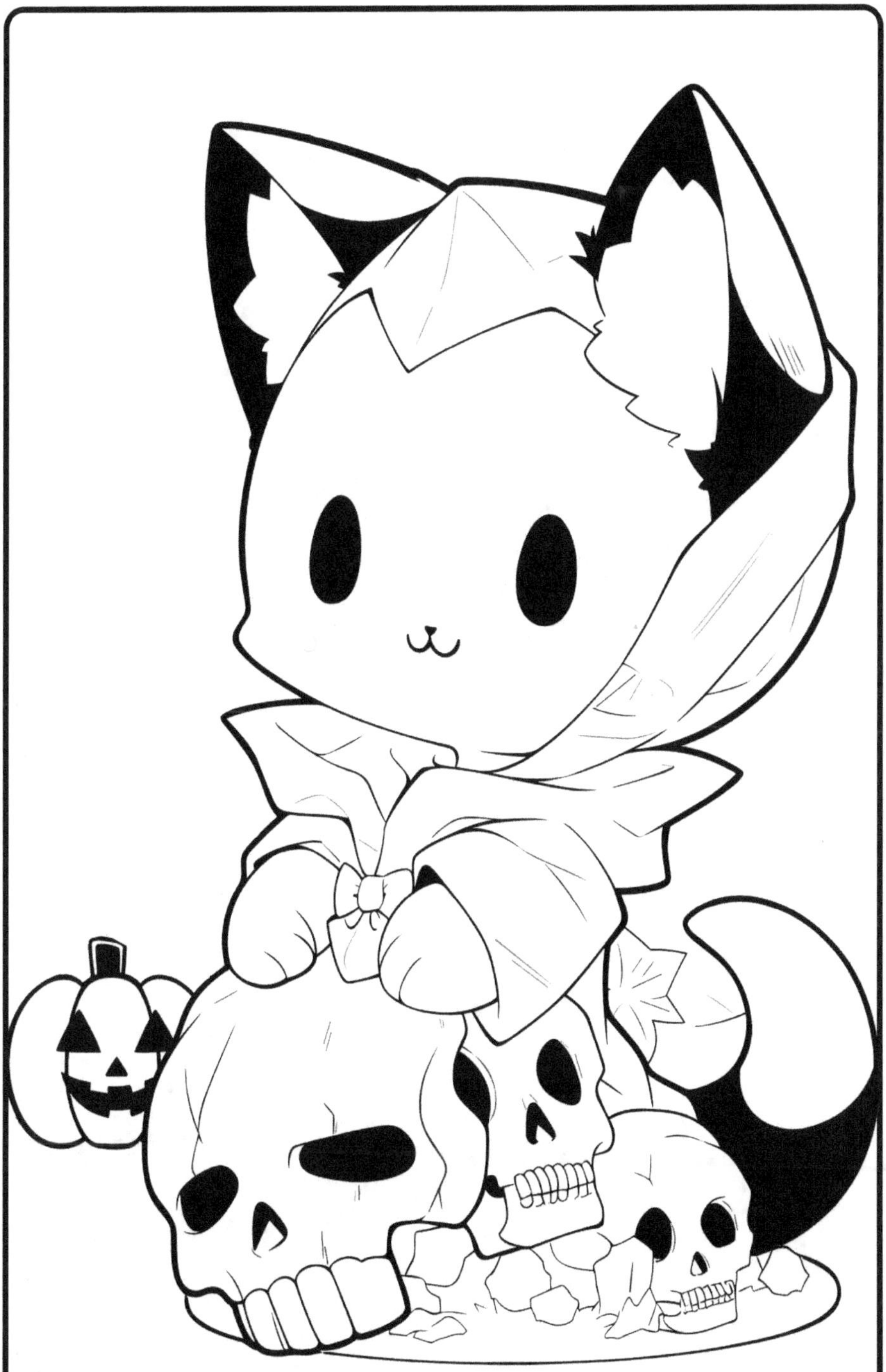

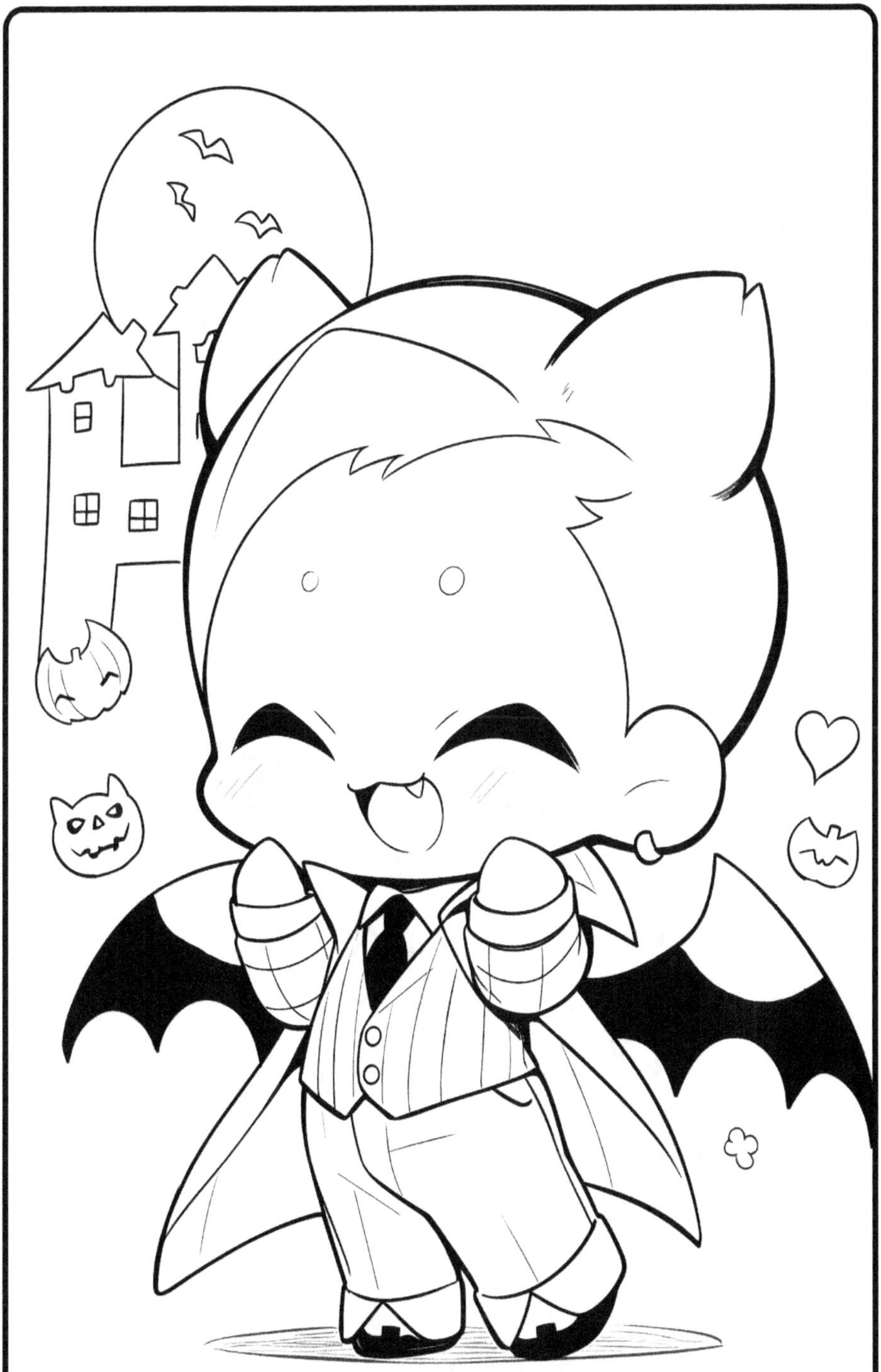

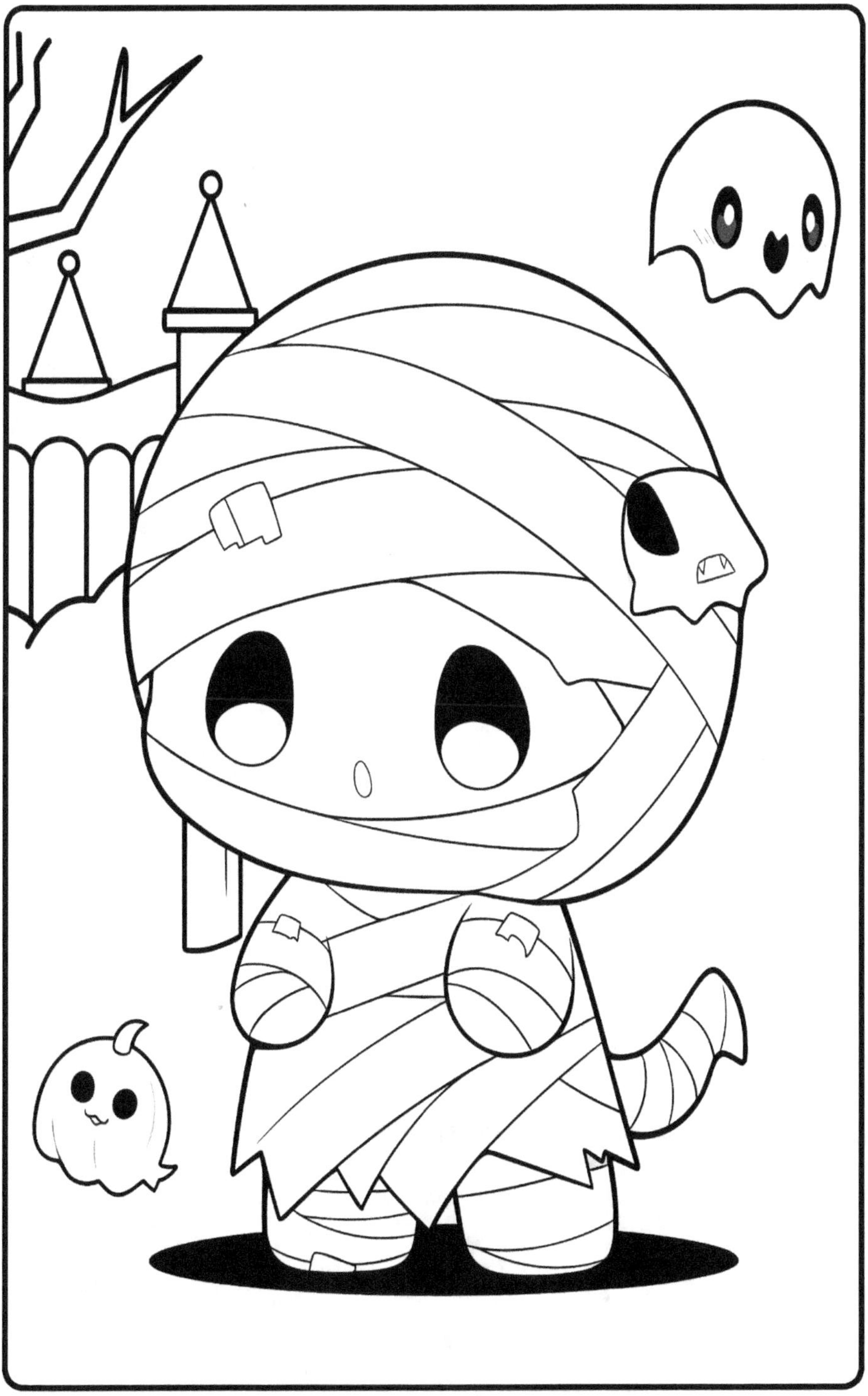

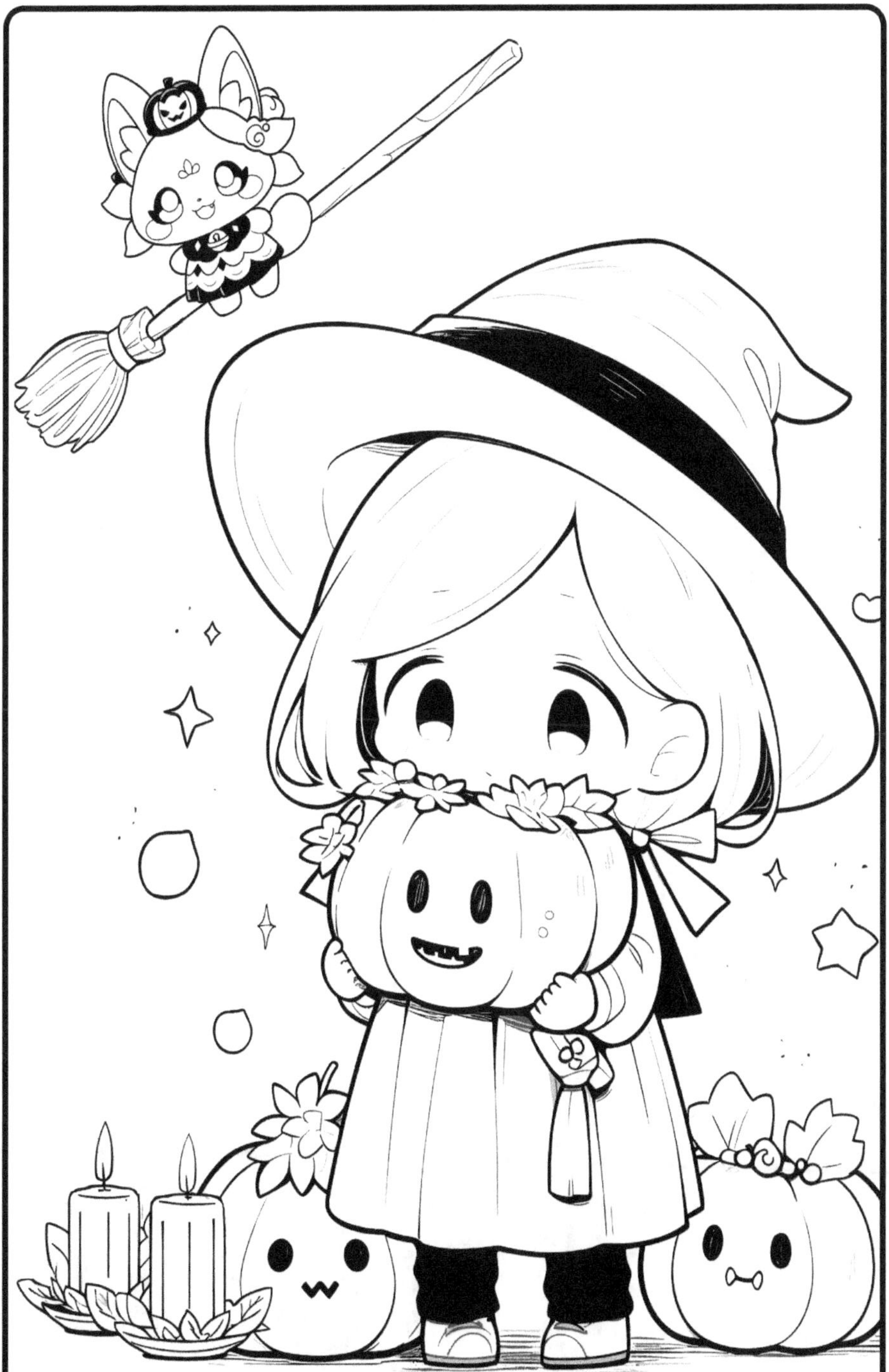

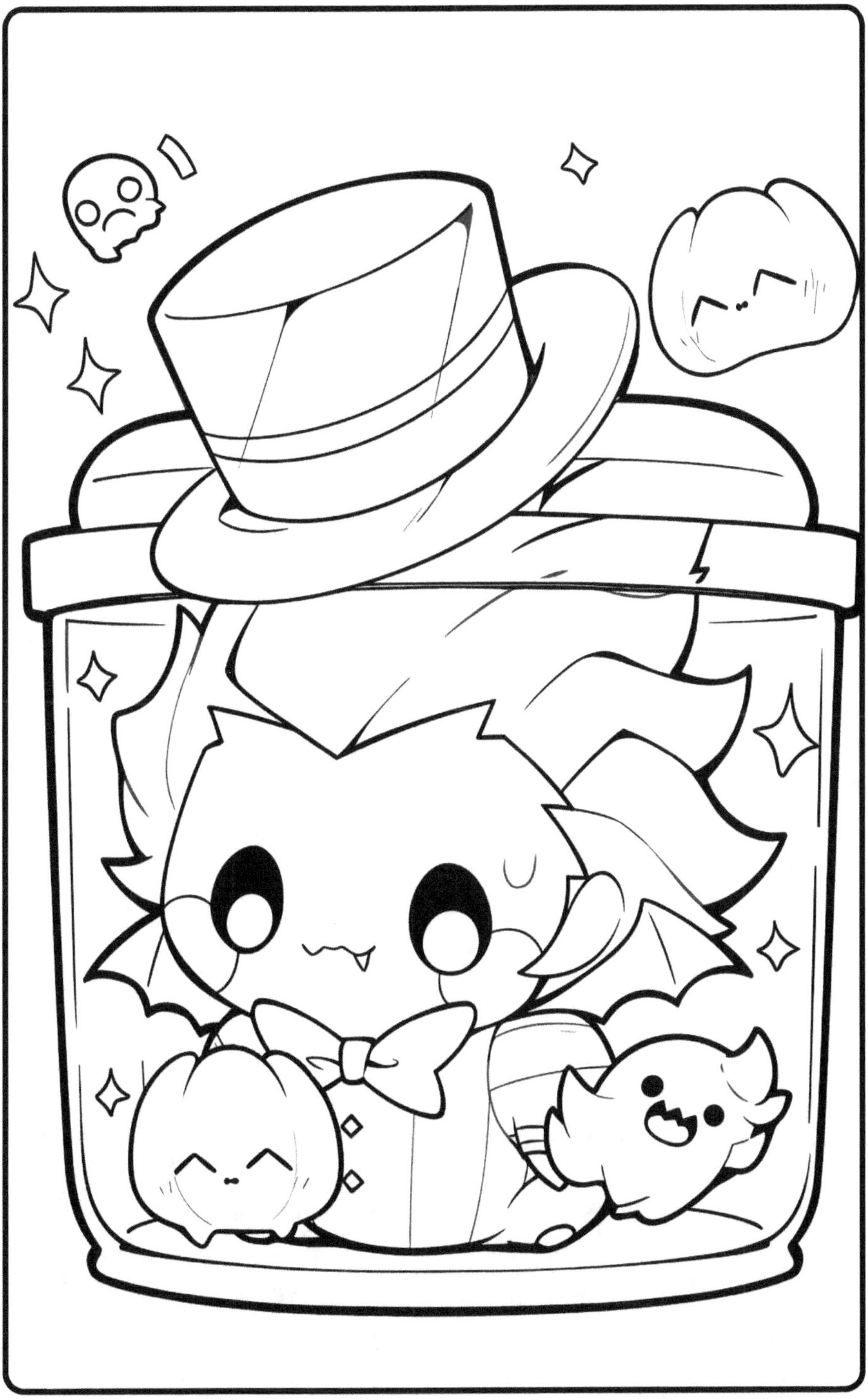

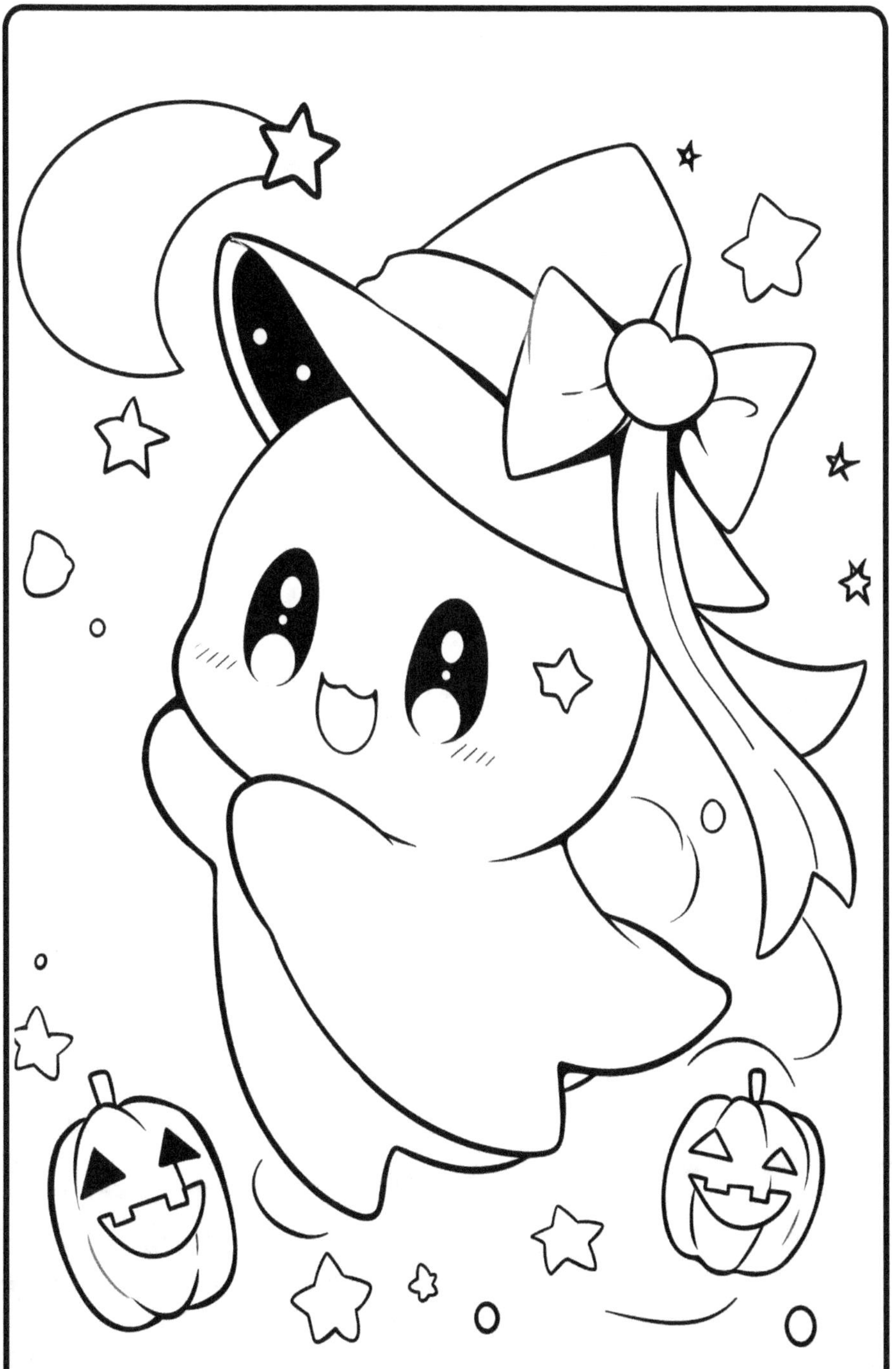

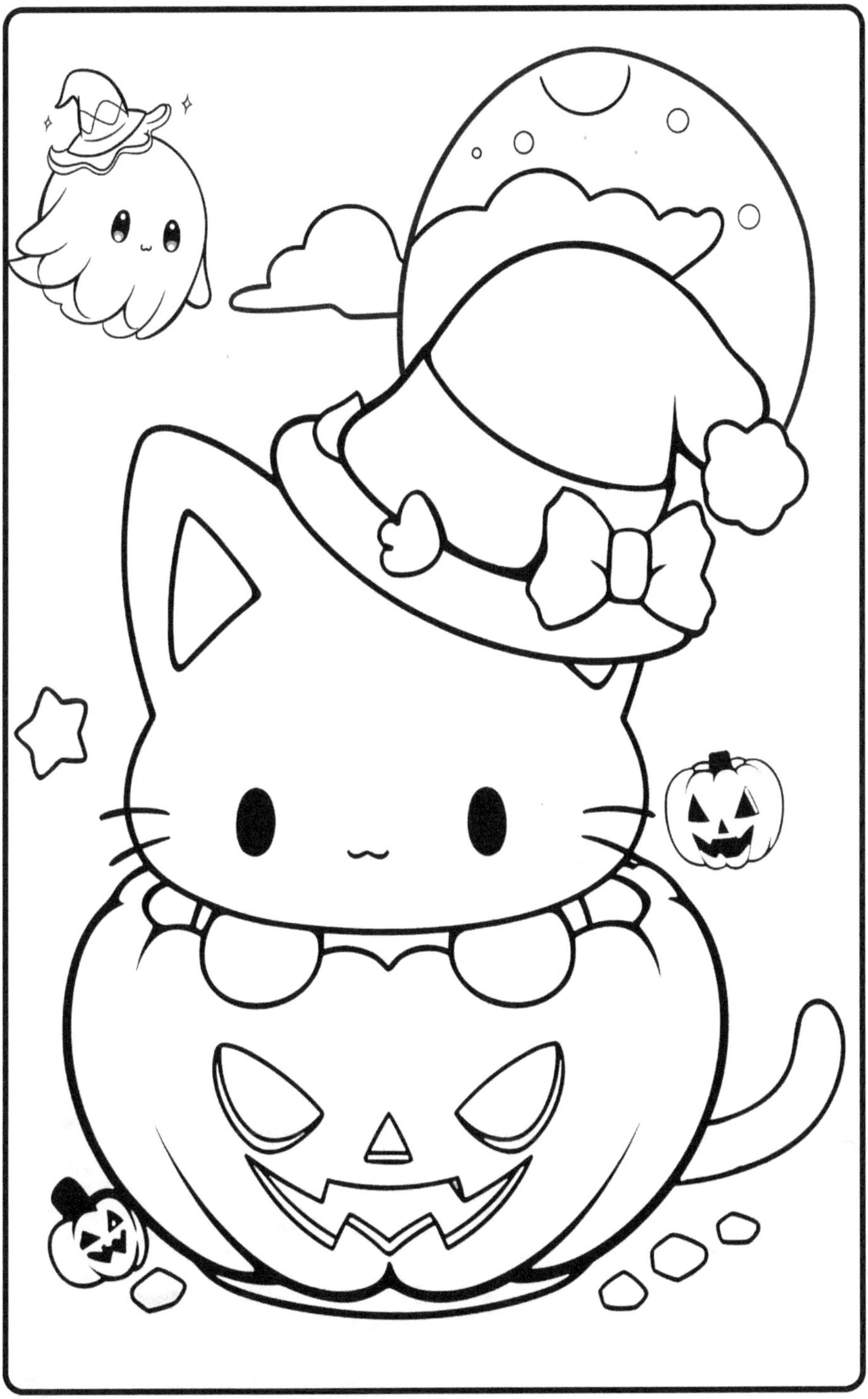

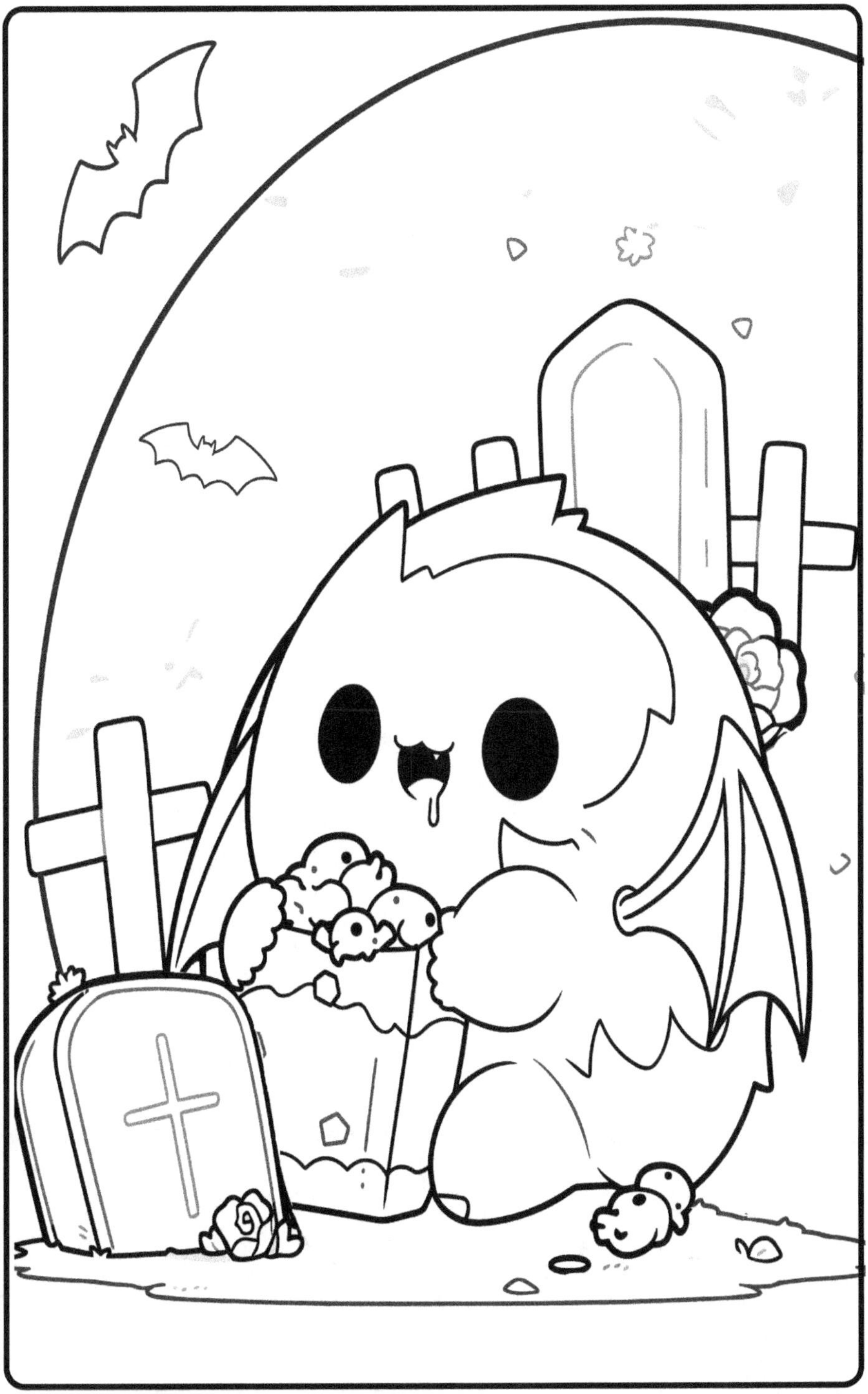

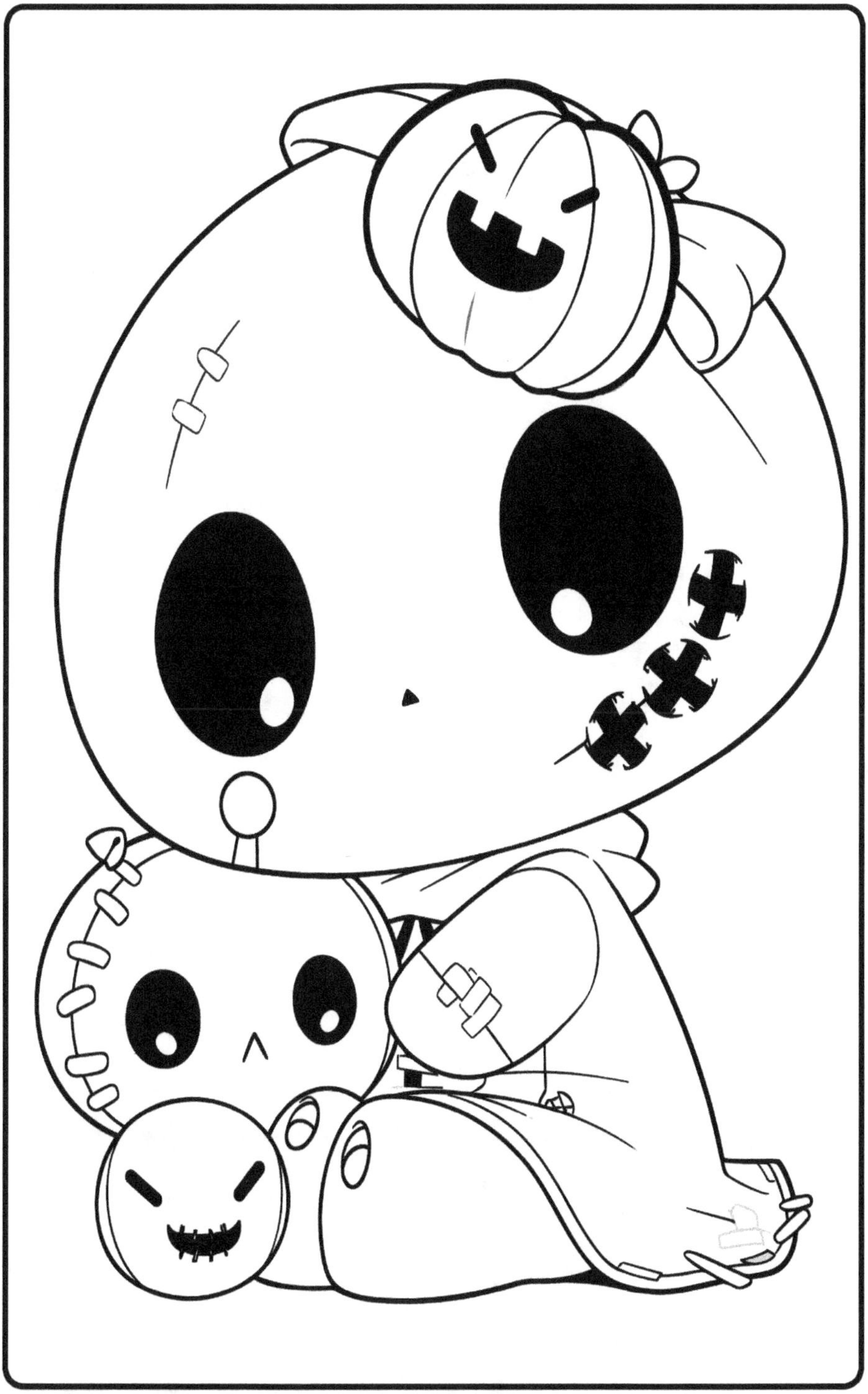

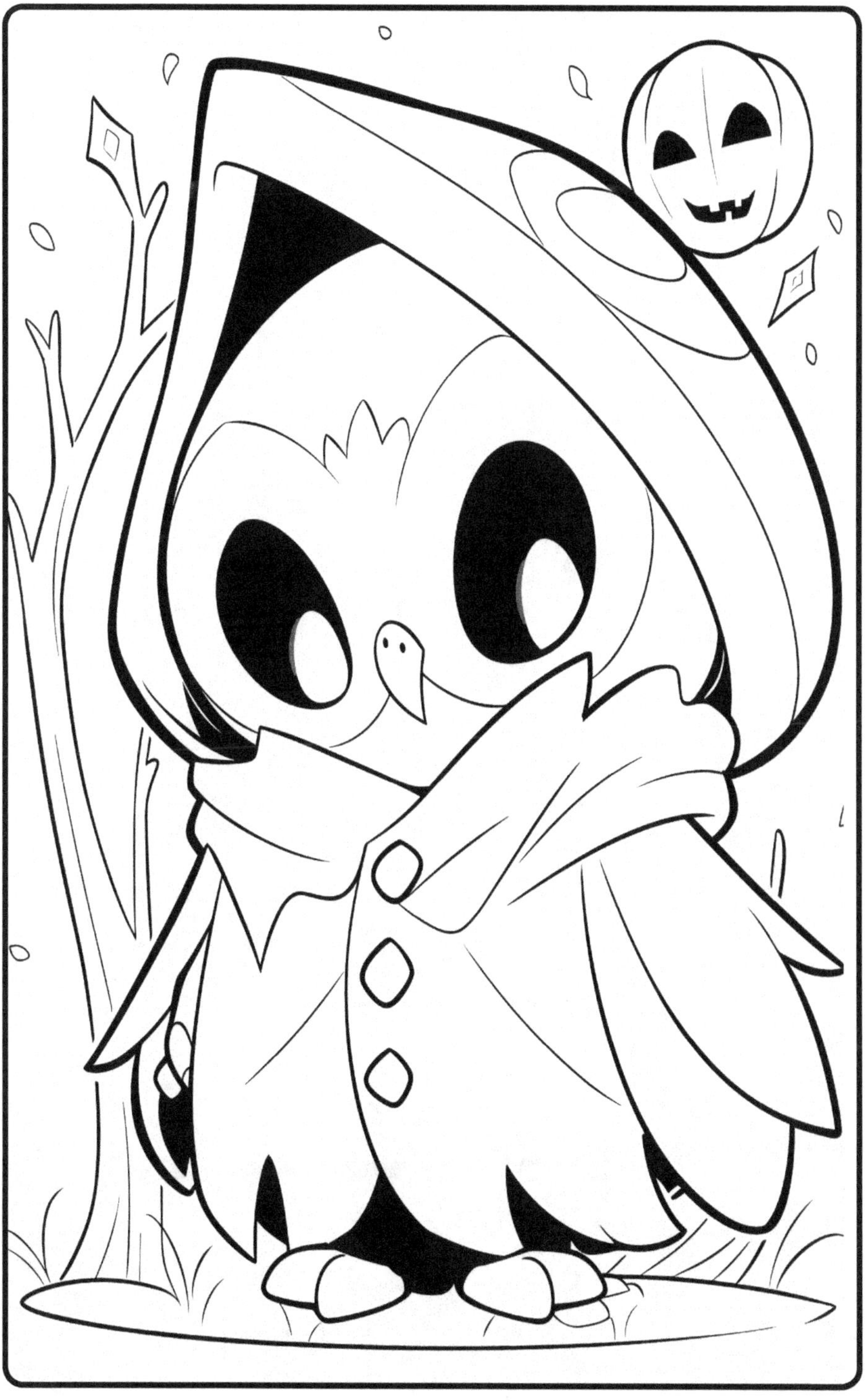

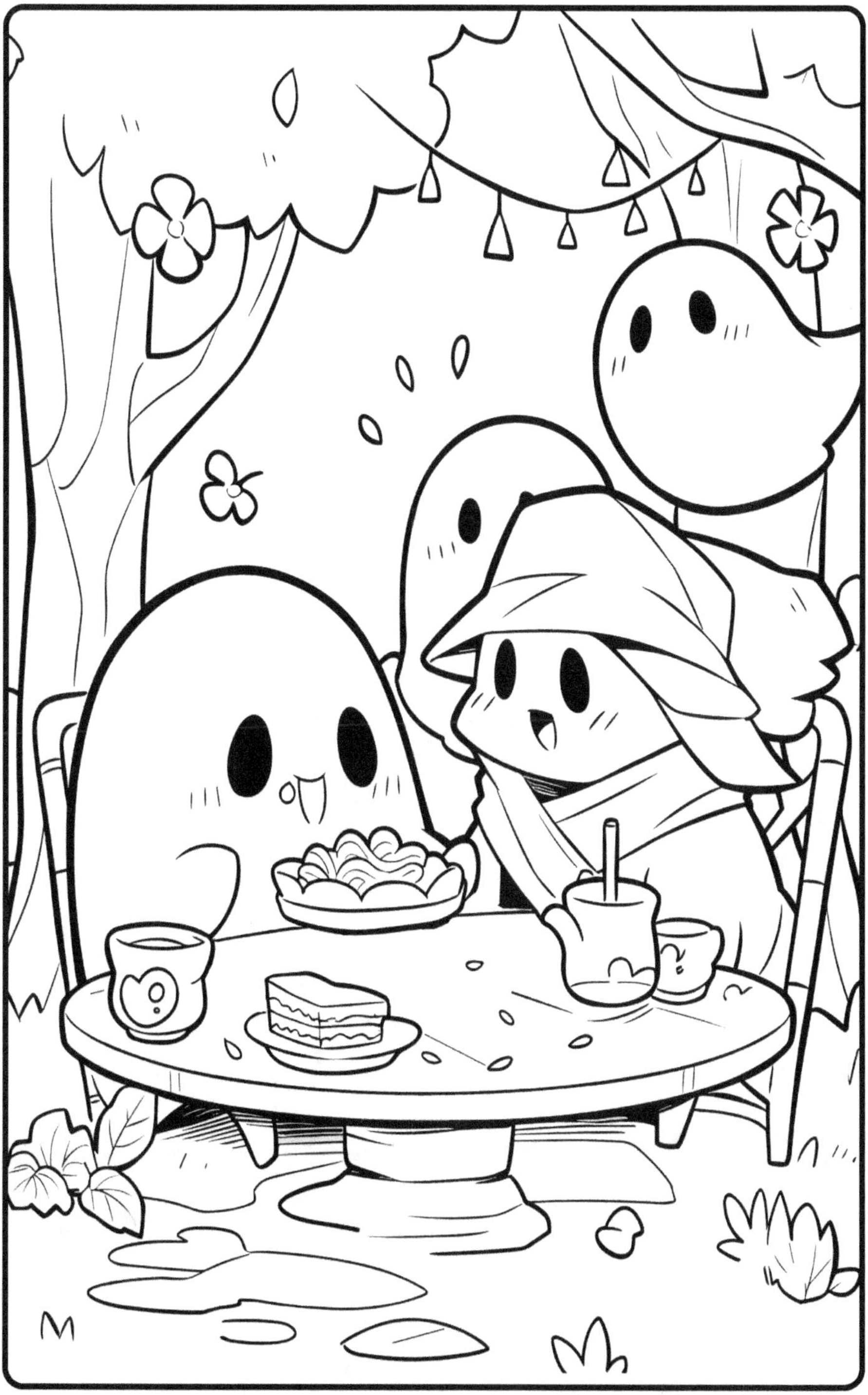

www.ingramcontent.com/pod-product-compliance
Lightning Source LLC
Chambersburg PA
CBHW060009300526
45794CB00003B/1155
9798858874218